T0065926

ANOTHER F★CKING

Coloring Book

Adams Media
New York London Toronto Sydney New Delhi

Adams Media
An Imprint of Simon & Schuster, Inc.
100 Technology Center Drive
Stoughton, MA 02072

Copyright © 2016 by Simon & Schuster, Inc.

All rights reserved, including the right to reproduce this book or portions thereof in any form whatsoever. For information address Adams Media Subsidiary Rights Department, 1230 Avenue of the Americas, New York, NY 10020.

ADAMS MEDIA and colophon are trademarks of Simon and Schuster.

For information about special discounts for bulk purchases, please contact Simon & Schuster Special Sales at 1-866-506-1949 or business@simonandschuster.com.

The Simon & Schuster Speakers Bureau can bring authors to your live event. For more information or to book an event contact the Simon & Schuster Speakers Bureau at 1-866-248-3049 or visit our website at www.simonspeakers.com.

Interior design by Michelle Roy Kelly
Interior images © iStockphoto.com

Manufactured in the United States of America

11 2022

Library of Congress Cataloging-in-Publication Data has been applied for.

ISBN 978-1-4405-9841-8

Many of the designations used by manufacturers and sellers to distinguish their products are claimed as trademarks. Where those designations appear in this book and Simon & Schuster, Inc., was aware of a trademark claim, the designations have been printed with initial capital letters.

BITCH, PLEASE

Image © iStockphoto.com/KUO CHUN HUNG

well aren't you just a fucking ray of sunshine?

Image © iStockphoto.com/artplay711

Life Sucks
then
you
Die

Image © iStockphoto.com/AlisaFoytik

HOME IS WHERE THE LIQUOR IS

Image © iStockphoto.com/KUO CHUN HUNG

today
blows

Image © iStockphoto.com/iveta cocks

ZONE
the fuck
OUT

Image © iStockphoto.com/i_panki

IT'S TEA TIME, BITCHES

Image © iStockphoto.com/KUO CHUN HUNG

YOU'RE ALL
A BUNCH OF SHEEP

Image © iStockphoto.com/librebird

Life
GET ONE

Image © iStockphoto.com/karakotsya

WHO THE FUCK ARE YOU?

Image © iStockphoto.com/KUO CHUN HUNG

DON'T BE

A PRICK

Image © iStockphoto.com/i_panki

chill af

Image © iStockphoto.com/saemilee

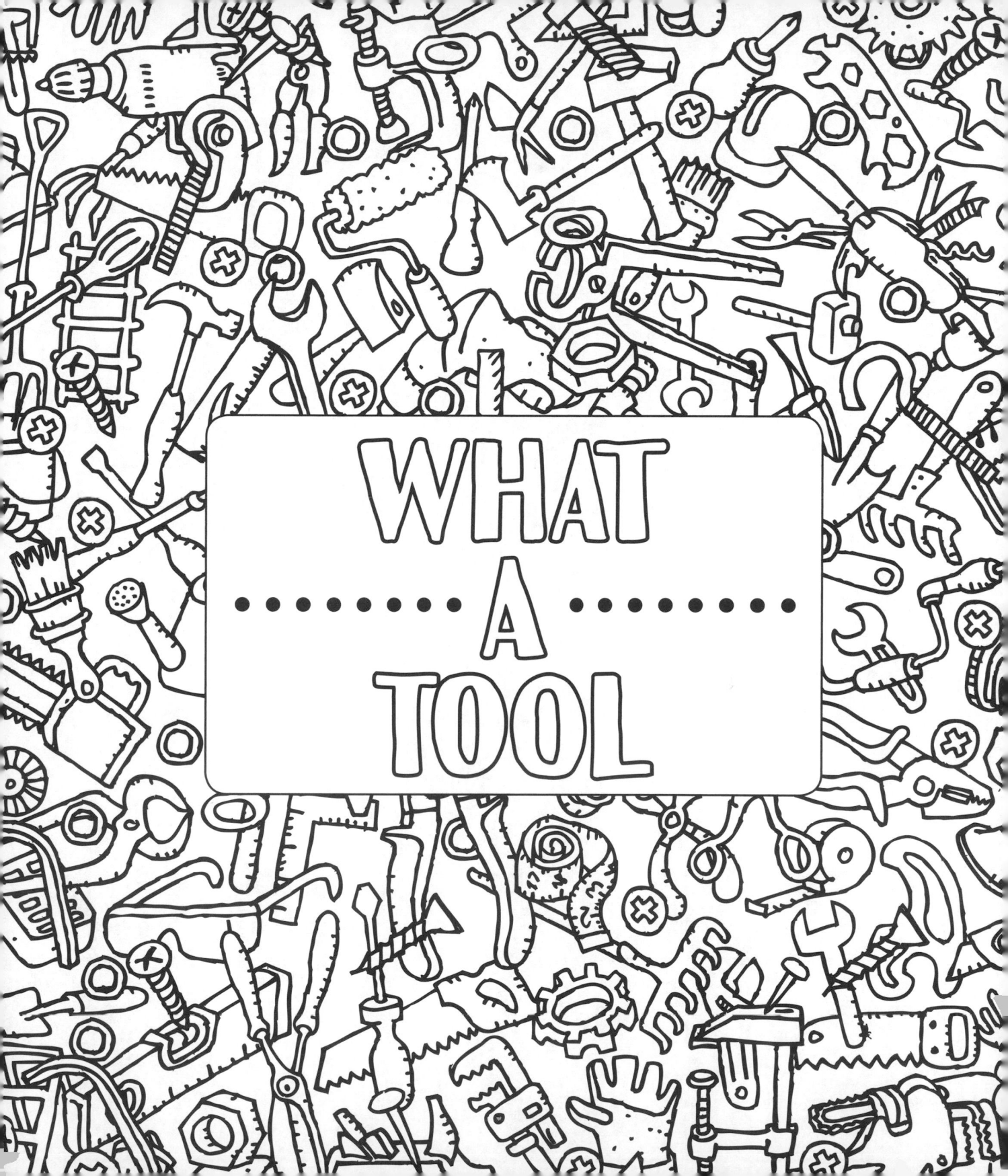
WHAT
A
TOOL

Image © iStockphoto.com/iVOOK

I
LICKED
ONE

Image © iStockphoto.com/elfiny

BOOKS ARE
FOR NERDS,
NERD

Image © iStockphoto.com/elfiny

what an ass

Image © iStockphoto.com/larisakuzovkova

WHOSE NUTS?

DEEZ NUTS!

Image © iStockphoto.com/KUO CHUN HUNG

I FARTED

Image © iStockphoto.com/i_panki

HAVE A GREAT DAY,
YOU WORTHLESS
TURD

Image © iStockphoto.com/mishkom

HANG IN
THERE,
ASSHOLE

Image © iStockphoto.com/Bimbimkha007

fuck this shit

Image © iStockphoto.com/Maria_Galybina

just
spreading
my seed

Image © iStockphoto.com/KavalenkavaVolha

FU

Image © iStockphoto.com/Daria_Volyanskaya and i_panki

YOU'RE
UNBEARABLE

Image © iStockphoto.com/Bimbimkha007

NOW THAT'S SOME BULL

Image © iStockphoto.com/YAZZIK

Are you high . . .
or just stupid?

Image © iStockphoto.com/i_panki

UNICORNS ARE FUCKING RAD

Image © iStockphoto.com/KUO CHUN HUNG

Eat Me

Image © iStockphoto.com/lexver

PLAYING WITH MY BALLS

Image © iStockphoto.com/AlexanderPokusay

I love you like a
fat kid loves cake

Image © iStockphoto.com/KatBuslaeva

Size
Matters

Image © iStockphoto.com/HelenaKrivoruchko

THREE
OF THESE
PEOPLE
WILL BE
DEAD
TOMORROW

Image © iStockphoto.com/Golderuna

ENJOY YOUR TRIP

Image © iStockphoto.com/KUO CHUN HUNG

Rainbows
make me barf

Image © iStockphoto.com/blue67

JUNK
IN
THE
TRUNK

Image © iStockphoto.com/TopVectors

someone
loves
you
but it's not me

Image © iStockphoto.com/blue67

COFFEE OR HOMICIDE

Image © iStockphoto.com/Vyazovskaya_Julia

if a tree falls in the woods, does anyone give a damn?

Image © iStockphoto.com/Maria_Galybina

GO
AWAY

Image © iStockphoto.com/KUO CHUN HUNG

YOU'RE
UGLY AS
FUCK

Image © iStockphoto.com/kchungtw

SUCK
IT
SUCK
IT

Image © iStockphoto.com/tasza_natasha

DON'T RAIN ON MY FUCKING PARADE

Image © iStockphoto.com/KUO CHUN HUNG

DRINK
LIKE
NO
ONE
IS WATCHING
WHISKEY
1866
40%

Image © iStockphoto.com/chekat

your words
are like air
from a colon

Image © iStockphoto.com/KUO CHUN HUNG

'SUP BEEYOTCH

Image © iStockphoto.com/lenkis_art and inides

in wine there is
wisdom,
in beer there is
freedom,
in water there is
bacteria

Image © iStockphoto.com/Zalevna

BUGGIN'
OUT

Image © iStockphoto.com/KsanasK